The Invention of a

New Religion

Basil Hall Chamberlain

Contents

THE INVENTION OF
A NEW RELIGION

BY

Basil Hall Chamberlain

THE INVENTION OF A NEW RELIGION BY B. H.
CHAMBERLAIN, EMERITUS PROFESSOR OF
JAPANESE AND PHILOLOGY AT THE IMPERIAL
UNIVERSITY OF TOKYO, JAPAN 1912

The Invention of a New Religion[1]

Voltaire and the other eighteenth-century philosophers, who held religions to be the invention of priests, have been scorned as superficial by later investigators. But was there not something in their view, after all? Have not we, of a later and more critical day, got into so inveterate a habit of digging deep that we sometimes fail to see what lies before our very noses? Modern Japan is there to furnish an example. The Japanese are, it is true, commonly said to be an irreligious people. They say so themselves. Writes one of them, the celebrated Fukuzawa, teacher and type of the modern educated Japanese man: "I lack a religious nature, and have never believed in any religion." A score of like pronouncements might be quoted from other leading men. The average, even educated, European strikes the average educated Japanese as strangely superstitious, unaccountably occupied with supra-mundane matters. The Japanese simply cannot be brought to comprehend how a "mere parson" such as the Pope, or even the Archbishop of Canterbury, occupies the place he does in politics and society. Yet this same agnostic Japan is teaching us at this very

---

1   The writer of this pamphlet could but
skim over a wide subject. For full information see
Volume I. of Mr. J. Murdoch's recently-published
"History of Japan," the only critical work on that
subject existing in the English language.

hour how religions are sometimes manufactured for a special end--to subserve practical worldly purposes.

Mikado-worship and Japan-worship--for that is the new Japanese religion--is, of course, no spontaneously generated phenomenon. Every manufacture presupposes a material out of which it is made, every present a past on which it rests. But the twentieth-century Japanese religion of loyalty and patriotism is quite new, for in it pre-existing ideas have been sifted, altered, freshly compounded, turned to new uses, and have found a new centre of gravity. Not only is it new, it is not yet completed; it is still in process of being consciously or semi-consciously put together by the official class, in order to serve the interests of that class, and, incidentally, the interests of the nation at large. The Japanese bureaucracy is a body greatly to be admired. It includes most of the foremost men of the nation. Like the priesthood in later Judaea, to some extent like the Egyptian and Indian priesthoods, it not only governs, but aspires to lead in intellectual matters. It has before it a complex task. On the one hand, it must make good to the outer world the new claim that Japan differs in no essential way from the nations of the West, unless, indeed, it be by way of superiority. On the other hand, it has to manage restive steeds at home, where ancestral ideas and habits clash with new dangers arising from an alien material civilisation hastily absorbed.

Down to the year 1888, the line of cleavage between governors and governed was obscured by the joyful ardour with which all classes alike devoted themselves to the acquisition of European, not to say American, ideas. Everything foreign was then hailed as perfect--everything old and national was contemned. Sentiment grew democratic, in so far (perhaps it was not very far) as American democratic ideals were understood. Love of country seemed likely to yield to a humble bowing down before foreign models. Officialdom not unnaturally took fright at this abdication of national individualism. Evidently something must be done to turn the tide. Accordingly, patriotic sentiment was appealed to through the throne, whose hoary antiquity had ever been a source of pride to Japanese literati, who loved to dwell on the contrast between Japan's unique line of absolute monarchs and the short-lived dynasties of China. Shinto, a primitive nature cult, which had fallen into discredit, was taken out of its cupboard and dusted. The common people, it is true, continued to place their affections on Buddhism, the popular festivals were Buddhist, Buddhist also the temples where they buried their dead. The governing class determined to change all this. They insisted on the Shinto doctrine that the Mikado descends in direct succession from the native Goddess of the Sun, and that He himself is a living God on earth who justly claims the absolute fealty of his subjects. Such things as laws and constitutions are but free gifts on His part, not in any sense popular rights. Of course, the ministers and officials, high and low, who carry on His government, are to be regarded not as public servants, but rather as executants of supreme--one might say supernatural--authority. Shinto, because connected with the Imperial Family, is to be alone honoured. Therefore, the important right of burial, never before possessed by it, was granted to its priests. Later on, the right of marriage was granted likewise--an entirely novel departure in a land where marriage had never been more than a civil contract. Thus the Shinto priesthood was encouraged to penetrate into the intimacy of family life, while in another direction it encroached on the field of ethics by borrowing bits here and there from Confucian and even from Christian sources. Under a regime of ostensible religious toleration, the attendance of officials at certain Shinto services was required, and the practice was established in all schools of bowing down several times yearly before the Emperor's picture. Meanwhile Japanese polities had prospered; her warriors had gained great victories. Enormous was the prestige thus accruing to Imperialism and to the rejuvenated Shinto cult. All military successes were ascribed to the miraculous influence of the Emperor's virtue, and to the virtues of His Imperial and divine ancestors--that is, of former Emperors and of Shinto deities. Imperial envoys were regularly sent after each great victory to carry the good tidings to the Sun Goddess at her great shrine at Ise. Not there alone, but at the other principal Shinto shrines throughout the land, the cannon captured from Chinese or Russian foes were officially installed, with a view to identifying Imperialism, Shinto, and national glory in the popular mind. The new legend is enforced wherever feasible--for instance, by means of a new set of festivals celebrating Imperial official events.

But the schools are the great strongholds of the new propaganda. History is so taught to the young as to focus everything upon Imperialism, and to diminish as far as possible the contrast between ancient and modern conditions. The same is true of the instruction given to army and navy recruits. Thus, though Shinto is put in the forefront, little stress is laid on its mythology, which would be apt to shock even the Japanese mind at the present day. To this extent, where a purpose useful to the ruling class is to be served, criticism is practised, though not avowedly. Far different is the case with so-called "historical facts," such as the alleged foundation of the Monarchy in 660 B.C. and similar statements paralleled only for absurdity by what passed for history in mediaeval Europe, when King Lear, Brute, King of Britain, etc., etc., were accepted as authentic personages. For the truth, known to all critical investigators, is that, instead of going back to a remote antiquity, the origins of Japanese history are recent as compared with that of European countries. The first glimmer of genuine Japanese history dates from the fifth century AFTER Christ, and even the accounts of what happened in the sixth century must be received with caution. Japanese scholars know this as well as we do; it is one of the certain results of investigation. But the Japanese bureaucracy does not desire to have the light let in on this inconvenient circumstance. While granting a dispensation re the national mythology, properly so called, it exacts belief in every iota of the national historic legends. Woe to the native professor who strays from the path of orthodoxy. His wife and children (and in Japan every man, however young, has a wife and children) will starve. From the late Prince Ito's grossly misleading "Commentary on the Japanese Constitution" down to school compendiums, the absurd dates are everywhere insisted upon. This despite the fact that the mythology and the so-called early history are recorded in the same works, and are characterised by like miraculous impossibilities; that the chronology is palpably fraudulent; that the speeches put into the mouths of ancient Mikados are centos culled from the Chinese classics; that their names are in some cases derived from Chinese sources; and that the earliest Japanese historical narratives, the earliest known social usages, and even the centralised Imperial form of Government itself, are all stained through and through with a Chinese dye, so much so that it is no longer possible to determine what percentage of old native thought may still linger on in fragments here and there. In the face of all this, moral ideals, which were of common knowledge derived from the teaching of the Chinese sages, are now arbitrarily referred to the "Imperial Ancestors." Such, in particular, are loyalty and filial piety--the two virtues on which, in the Far-Eastern world, all the others rest. It is, furthermore, officially taught that, from the earliest ages, perfect concord has always subsisted in Japan between beneficent sovereigns on the one hand, and a gratefully loyal people on the other. Never, it is alleged, has Japan been soiled by the disobedient and rebellious acts common in other countries; while at the same time the Japanese nation, sharing to some extent in the supernatural virtues of its rulers, has been distinguished by a high-minded chivalry called Bushido, unknown in inferior lands.

Such is the fabric of ideas which the official class is busy building up by every means in its power, including the punishment of those who presume to stickle for historic truth.

*   *   *

The sober fact is that no nation probably has ever treated its sovereigns more cavalierly than the Japanese have done, from the beginning of authentic history down to within the memory of living men. Emperors have been deposed, emperors have been assassinated; for centuries every succession to the throne was the signal for intrigues and sanguinary broils. Emperors have been exiled; some have been murdered in exile. From the remote island to which he had been relegated one managed to escape, hidden under a load of dried fish. In the fourteenth century, things came to such a pass that two rival Imperial lines defied each other for the space of fifty-eight years-- the so-called Northern and Southern Courts; and it was the Northern Court, branded by later historians as usurping and illegitimate, that ultimately won the day, and handed on the Imperial regalia to its successors. After that, as indeed before that, for long centuries the government was in the hands of Mayors of the Palace, who substituted one infant Sovereign for another, generally forcing each to abdicate as soon as he approached man's estate. At one period, these Mayors of the Palace left the Descendant of the Sun in such distress that His Imperial Majesty and the Imperial Princes were obliged to gain a livelihood by selling their autographs! Nor did any

great party in the State protest against this condition of affairs. Even
in the present reign--the most glorious in Japanese history--there have
been two rebellions, during one of which a rival Emperor was set up in
one part of the country, and a republic proclaimed in another.

As for Bushido, so modern a thing is it that neither Kaempfer, Sie-
bold, Satow, nor Rein--all men knowing their Japan by heart --ever
once allude to it in their voluminous writings. The cause of their si-
lence is not far to seek: Bushido was unknown until a decade or two
ago! THE VERY WORD APPEARS IN NO DICTIONARY, NATIVE
OR FOREIGN, BEFORE THE YEAR 1900. Chivalrous individuals of
course existed in Japan, as in all countries at every period; but Bushido,
as an institution or a code of rules, has never existed. The accounts
given of it have been fabricated out of whole cloth, chiefly for foreign
consumption. An analysis of medieval Japanese history shows that the
great feudal houses, so far from displaying an excessive idealism in the
matter of fealty to one emperor, one lord, or one party, had evolved the
eminently practical plan of letting their different members take different sides, so that the family as a whole might come out as winner in
any event, and thus avoid the confiscation of its lands. Cases, no doubt,
occurred of devotion to losing causes--for example, to Mikados in dis-
grace; but they were less common than in the more romantic West.

Thus, within the space of a short lifetime, the new Japanese religion
of loyalty and patriotism has emerged into the light of day. The feats
accomplished during the late war with Russia show that the simple ideal
which it offers is capable of inspiring great deeds. From a certain point
of view the nation may be congratulated on its new possession.

*   *   *

The new Japanese religion consists, in its present early stage, of worship of the sacrosanct Imperial Person and of His Divine Ancestors, of implicit obedience to Him as head of the army (a position, by the way, opposed to all former Japanese ideas, according to which the Court was essentially civilian); furthermore, of a corresponding belief that Japan is as far superior to the common ruck of nations as the Mikado is divinely superior to the common ruck of kings and emperors. Do not the early history-books record the fact that Japan was created first, while all other countries resulted merely from the drops that fell from the creator's spear when he had finished his main work? And do not the later annals prove that true valour belongs to the Japanese knight alone, whereas foreign countries--China and Europe alike--are sunk in a degrading commercialism? For the inhabitants of "the Land of the Gods" to take any notice of such creatures by adopting a few of their trifling mechanical inventions is an act of gracious condescension.

To quote but one official utterance out of a hundred, Baron Oura, minister of agriculture and commerce, writes thus in February of last year:--

> That the majesty of our Imperial House towers high
> above everything to be found in the world, and that
> it is as durable as heaven and earth, is too well
> known to need dwelling on here...... If it is
> considered that our country needs a religious faith,
> then, I say, let it be converted to a belief in the
> religion of patriotism and loyalty, the religion of

Imperialism--in other words, to Emperor-worship.

The Rev. Dr. Ebina[2], one of the leading lights of the Protestant pastorate in Japan, plunges more deeply still into this doctrine, according to which, as already noted, the whole Japanese nation is, in a manner, apotheosised. Says he:--

> Though the encouragement of ancestor-worship cannot
> be regarded as part of the essential teaching of
> Christianity (!), it[3] is not opposed to the
> notion that, when the Japanese Empire was founded,
> its early rulers were in communication with the
> Great Spirit that rules the universe. Christians,
> according to this theory, without doing violence
> to their creed, may acknowledge that the Japanese
> nation has a divine origin. It is only when we
> realise that the Imperial Ancestors were in close
> communion with God (or the Gods), that we understand
> how sacred is the country in which we live[4].

It needs no comment of ours to point out how thoroughly the nation must be saturated by the doctrines under discussion for such amazing utterances to be possible. If so-called Christians can think thus, the

2   We quote from the translation given by Mr. Walter Dening in one of the invaluable "Summaries of Current Japanese Literature," contributed by him from time to time to the columns of the "Japan Mail," Yokohama.

3   "It" means Christianity.

4   Dr. Ebina ends by recommending the Imperial Rescript on Education as a text for Christian sermons.

non-Christian majority must indeed be devout Emperor-worshippers and Japan-worshippers. Such the go-ahead portion of the nation un-doubtedly is--the students, the army, the navy, the emigrants to Japan's new foreign possessions, all the more ardent spirits. The peasantry, as before noted, occupy themselves little with new thoughts, clinging rather to the Buddhist beliefs of their forefathers. But nothing could be further removed from even their minds than the idea of offering any organised resistance to the propaganda going on around them.

As a matter of fact, the spread of the new ideas has been easy, be-cause a large class derives power from their diffusion, while to oppose them is the business of no one in particular. Moreover, the disinter-ested love of truth for its own sake is rare; the patience to unearth it is rarer still, especially in the East. Patriotism, too, is a mighty engine working in the interests of credulity. How should men not believe in a system that produces such excellent practical results, a system which has united all the scattered elements of national feeling into one focus, and has thus created a powerful instrument for the attainment of na-tional aims? Meanwhile a generation is growing up which does not so much as suspect that its cherished beliefs are inventions of yesterday.

The new religion, in its present stage, still lacks one important item--a sacred book. Certain indications show that this lacuna will be filled by the elevation of the more important Imperial Rescripts to that rank, accompanied doubtless by an authoritative commentary, as their style is too abstruse to be understanded of the people. To these Imperial Rescripts some of the poems composed by his present Majesty may be added. In fact, a volume on the whole duty of Japanese man, with se-lected Imperial poems as texts, has already appeared[5].

---

5 For over a thousand years the composition of Japanese and Chinese verse has formed part of a liberal education, like the composition of Latin verse among ourselves. The Court has always

* * *

One might have imagined that Japan's new religionists would have experienced some difficulty in persuading foreign nations of the truth of their dogmas. Things have fallen out otherwise. Europe and America evince a singular taste for the marvellous, and find a zest in self-depreciation. Our eighteenth-century ancestors imagined all perfections to be realised in China, thanks to the glowing descriptions then given of that country by the Jesuits. Twentieth-century Europe finds its moral and political Eldorado in distant Japan, a land of fabulous antiquity and incredible virtues. There is no lack of pleasant-mannered persons ready to guide trustful admirers in the right path. Official and semi- official Japanese, whether ambassadors and ministers-resident or peripatetic counts and barons, make it their business to spread a legend so pleasing to the national vanity, so useful as a diplomatic engine. Lectures are delivered, books are written in English, important periodicals are bought up, minute care is lavished on the concealment, the patching-up, and glossing-over of the deep gulf that nevertheless is fixed between East and West. The foreigner cannot refuse the bolus thus artfully forced down his throat. He is not suspicious by nature. How should he imagine that people who make such positive statements about their own country are merely exploiting his credulity? HE has reached a stage of culture where such mythopoeia has become impossible. On the other hand, to control information by consulting original sources lies beyond

devoted much time to the practice of this art. But the poems of former Emperors were little known, because the monarchs themselves remained shut up in their palace, and exercised no influence beyond its walls. With his present Majesty the case is entirely different. Moreover,some of his compositions breathe a patriotism formerly undreamt of.

his capacity.

For consider this peculiar circumstance: the position of European investigators vis-a-vis Japan differs entirely from that of Japanese vis-a-vis Europe. The Japanese possess every facility for studying and understanding Europe. Europeans are warded off by well-nigh insuperable obstacles from understanding Japan. Europe stands on a hill-top, in the sunlight, glittering afar. Her people court inspection. "Come and see how we live"--such was a typical invitation which the present writer recently received. A thousand English homes are open to any Japanese student or traveller who visits our shores. An alphabet of but six-and-twenty simple letters throws equally wide open to him a literature clearly revealing our thoughts, so that he who runs may read. Japan lies in the shadow, away on the rim of the world. Her houses are far more effectually closed to the stranger by their paper shutters than are ours by walls of brick or stone. What we call "society" does not exist there. Her people, though smiling and courteous, surround themselves by an atmosphere of reserve, centuries of despotic government having rendered them suspicious and reticent. True, when a foreigner of importance visits Japan--some British M.P., perhaps, whose name figures often in the newspapers, or an American editor, or the president of a great American college--this personage is charmingly received. But he is never left free to form his own opinion of things, even were he capable of so doing. Circumstances spin an invisible web around him, his hosts being keenly intent on making him a speaking-trumpet for the proclamation of their own views.

Again, Japan's non-Aryan speech, marvellously intricate, almost defies acquisition. Suppose this difficult vernacular mastered; the would-be student discovers that literary works, even newspapers and ordinary correspondence, are not composed in it, but in another dialect, partly antiquated, partly artificial, differing as widely from the colloquial speech as Latin does from Italian. Make a second hazardous supposition. Assume that the grammar and vocabulary of this second indispensable Japanese language have been learnt, in addition to the first. You are still but at the threshold of your task, Japanese thought having barricaded itself behind the fortress walls of an extraordinarily complicated system of writing, compared with which Egyptian hieroglyphics are child's play. Yet next to nothing can be found out by a foreigner unless he have this, too, at his fingers' ends. As a matter of fact, scarcely anyone acquires it--only a missionary here and there, or a consular official with a life appointment.

The result of all this is that, whereas the Japanese know everything that it imports them to know about us, Europeans cannot know much about them, such information as they receive being always belated, necessarily meagre, and mostly adulterated to serve Japanese interests. International relations placed--and, we repeat it, inevitably placed--on this footing resemble a boxing match in which one of the contestants should have his hands tied. But the metaphor fails in an essential point, as metaphors are apt to do--the hand-tied man does not realise the disadvantage under which he labours. He thinks himself as free as his opponent.

Thus does it come about that the neo-Japanese myths concerning dates, and Emperors, and heroes, and astonishing national virtues already begin to find their way into popular English text-books, current literature, and even grave books of reference. The Japanese governing class has willed it so, and in such matters the Japanese governing class can enforce its will abroad as well as at home. The statement may sound paradoxical. Study the question carefully, and you will find that it is simply true.

*   *   *

What is happening in Japan to-day is evidently exceptional. Normal religious and political change does not proceed in that manner; it proceeds by imperceptible degrees. But exceptions to general rules occur from time to time in every field of activity. Are they really exceptions, using that term in its current sense--to denote something arbitrary, and therefore unaccountable? Surely these so-called exceptions are but examples of rules of rarer application.

The classic instance of the invention of a new national religion is furnished by the Jews of the post-exilic period. The piecing together, then, of a brand-new system under an ancient name is now so well understood, and has produced consequences of such world-wide importance, that the briefest reference to it may suffice. Works which every critic can now see to be relatively modern were ascribed to Moses, David, or Daniel; intricate laws and ordinances that had never been practised-- could never be practised--were represented as ancient institutions; a whole new way of thinking and acting was set in motion on the assumption that it was old. Yet, so far as is known, no one in or out of Palestine ever saw through the illusion for over two thousand years. It was reserved for nineteenth-century scholars to draw aside the veil hiding the real facts of the case.

Modern times supply another instance, less important than the first, but remarkable enough. Rousseau came in the middle of the eighteenth century, and preached a doctrine that took the world by storm, and soon precipitated that world in ruins. How did he discover his gospel? He tells us quite naively:--

All the rest of the day, buried in the forest, I
sought, I found there the image of primitive ages,

whose history I boldly traced. I made havoc of men's
petty lies; I dared to unveil and strip naked man's
true nature, to follow up the course of time and of
the circumstances that have disfigured it, and,
comparing man as men have made him with man as
nature made him, to demonstrate that the so-called
improvements [of civilisation] have been the source
of all his woes, etc. [6]

In other words, he spun a pseudo-history from his own brain. What
is stranger, he fanatically believed in this his pure invention, and, most
extraordinary of all, persuaded other people to believe in it as fanatically. It was taken up as a religion, it inspired heroes, and enabled a
barefoot rabble to beat the finest regular armies in the world. Even
now, at a distance of a century and a half, its embers still glow.

Of course, it is not pretended that these various systems of thought
were ARBITRARY inventions. No more were they so than the cloud
palaces that we sometimes see swiftly form in the sky and as swiftly dis-
solve. The germ of Rousseau's ideas can be traced back to Fenelon and
other seventeenth-century thinkers, weary of the pomp and periwigs
around them. Rousseau himself did but fulfil the aspiration of a whole
society for something simpler, juster, more true to nature, more logi-
cal. He gave exactly what was needed at that moment of history-- what
appeared self-evident; wherefore no one so much as thought of asking
for detailed proofs. His deism, his statements concerning the "state of
nature" and the "social contract," etc., were at once recognised by the
people of his day as eternal verities. What need for discussion or inves-

6   "Confessions," Book VIII., year 1753.

tigation?

The case of Judaea is obscure; but it would seem that something analogous must have happened there, when the continuity of national life had been snapped by the exile. A revolutionised and most unhappy present involved a changed attitude towards the past. Oral tradition and the scraps of written records that had survived the shipwreck of the kingdom fell, as it were, naturally into another order. The kaleidoscope having been turned, the pattern changed of itself. A few gifted individuals voiced the enthusiasm of a whole community, when they adopted literary methods which would now, in our comparatively stable days, be branded as fraudulent. They simply could not help themselves. The pressing need of constructing a national polity for the present on the only basis then possible--Yahwe worship--FORCED them into falsifying the past. The question was one of life and death for the Jewish nationality.

*   *   *

Europeans there are in Japan--Europeanised Japanese likewise-- who feel outraged by the action of the Japanese bureaucracy in the matter of the new cult, with all the illiberal and obscurantist measures which it entails. That is natural. We modern Westerners love individual liberty, and the educated among us love to let the sunlight of criticism into every nook and cranny of every subject. Freedom and scientific accuracy are our gods. But Japanese officialdom acts quite naturally, after its kind, in not allowing the light to be let in, because the roots of the faith it has planted need darkness in which to grow and spread. No religion can live which is subjected to critical scrutiny.

Thus also are explained the rigours of the Japanese bureaucracy against the native liberals, who, in its eyes, appear, not simply as political opponents, but as traitors to the chosen people--sacrilegious heretics defying the authority of the One and Only True Church.

"But," you will say, "this indignation must be mere pretence. Not even officials can be so stupid as to believe in things which they have themselves invented." We venture to think that you are wrong here. People can always believe that which it is greatly to their interest to believe. Thousands of excellent persons in our own society cling to the doctrine of a future life on no stronger evidence. It is enormously important to the Japanese ruling class that the mental attitude sketched above should become universal among their countrymen. Accordingly, they achieve the apparently impossible. "We believe in it," said one of them to us recently--"we believe in it, although we know that it is not true." Tertullian said nearly the same thing, and no one has ever doubted HIS sincerity.

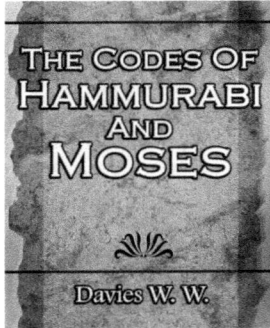

The Codes Of Hammurabi And Moses
W. W. Davies

QTY

The discovery of the Hammurabi Code is one of the greatest achievements of archaeology, and is of paramount interest, not only to the student of the Bible, but also to all those interested in ancient history...

Religion   **ISBN:** *1-59462-338-4*   **Pages:132**

MSRP $12.95

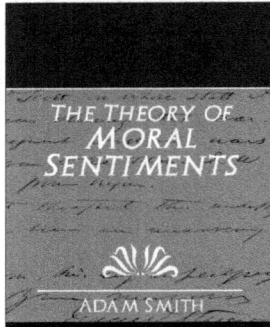

The Theory of Moral Sentiments
Adam Smith

QTY

This work from 1749. contains original theories of conscience amd moral judgment and it is the foundation for systemof morals.

Philosophy **ISBN:** *1-59462-777-0*   **Pages:536**

MSRP $19.95

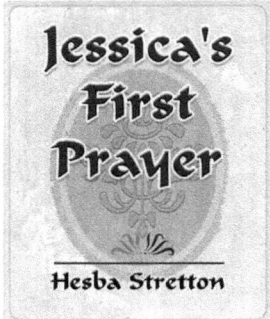

Jessica's First Prayer
Hesba Stretton

QTY

In a screened and secluded corner of one of the many railway-bridges which span the streets of London there could be seen a few years ago, from five o'clock every morning until half past eight, a tidily set-out coffee-stall, consisting of a trestle and board, upon which stood two large tin cans, with a small fire of charcoal burning under each so as to keep the coffee boiling during the early hours of the morning when the work-people were thronging into the city on their way to their daily toil...

Pages:84

Childrens   **ISBN:** *1-59462-373-2*   *MSRP $9.95*

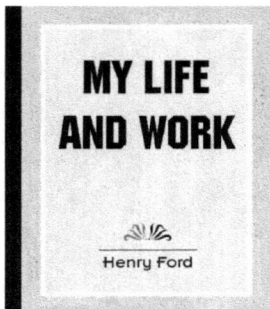

My Life and Work
Henry Ford

QTY

Henry Ford revolutionized the world with his implementation of mass production for the Model T automobile. Gain valuable business insight into his life and work with his own auto-biography... "We have only started on our development of our country we have not as yet, with all our talk of wonderful progress, done more than scratch the surface. The progress has been wonderful enough but..."

Pages:300

Biographies/   **ISBN:** *1-59462-198-5*   *MSRP $21.95*

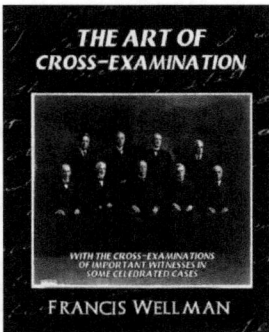

The Art of Cross-Examination
Francis Wellman

QTY

I presume it is the experience of every author, after his first book is published upon an important subject, to be almost overwhelmed with a wealth of ideas and illustrations which could readily have been included in his book, and which to his own mind, at least, seem to make a second edition inevitable. Such certainly was the case with me; and when the first edition had reached its sixth impression in five months, I rejoiced to learn that it seemed to my publishers that the book had met with a sufficiently favorable reception to justify a second and considerably enlarged edition. ..

Pages:412

Reference   ISBN: *1-59462-647-2*   *MSRP $19.95*

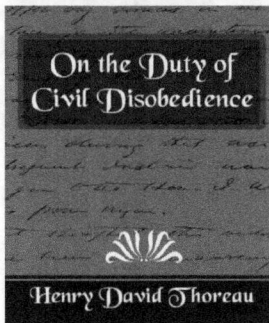

On the Duty of Civil Disobedience
Henry David Thoreau

QTY

Thoreau wrote his famous essay, On the Duty of Civil Disobedience, as a protest against an unjust but popular war and the immoral but popular institution of slave-owning. He did more than write—he declined to pay his taxes,   and was hauled off to gaol in consequence. Who can say how much this refusal of his hastened the end of the war and of slavery ?

Law   ISBN: *1-59462-747-9*   **Pages:48**

MSRP $7.45

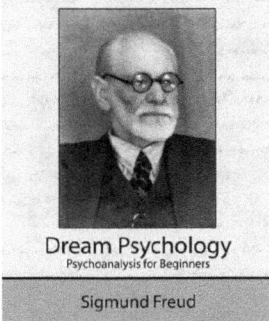

Dream Psychology Psychoanalysis for Beginners
Sigmund Freud

QTY

Sigmund Freud, born Sigismund Schlomo Freud (May 6, 1856 - September 23, 1939), was a Jewish-Austrian neurologist and psychiatrist who co-founded the psychoanalytic school of psychology. Freud is best known for his theories of the unconscious mind, especially involving the mechanism of repression; his redefinition of sexual desire as mobile and directed towards a wide variety of objects; and his therapeutic techniques, especially his understanding of transference in the therapeutic relationship and the presumed value of dreams as sources of insight into unconscious desires.

Pages:196

Psychology   ISBN: *1-59462-905-6*   *MSRP $15.45*

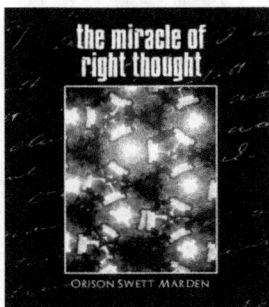

The Miracle of Right Thought
Orison Swett Marden

QTY

Believe with all of your heart that you will do what you were made to do. When the mind has once formed the habit of holding cheerful, happy, prosperous pictures, it will not be easy to form the opposite habit. It does not matter how improbable or how far away this realization may see, or how dark the prospects may be, if we visualize them as best we can, as vividly as possible, hold tenaciously to them and vigorously struggle to attain them, they will gradually become actualized, realized in the life. But a desire, a longing without endeavor, a yearning abandoned or held indifferently will vanish without realization.

Pages:360

Self Help   ISBN: *1-59462-644-8*   *MSRP $25.45*

QTY

The Rosicrucian Cosmo-Conception Mystic Christianity *by Max Heindel*   ISBN: *1-59462-188-8*   **$38.95**
The Rosicrucian Cosmo-conception is not dogmatic, neither does it appeal to any other authority than the reason of the student. It is: not controversial, but is: sent forth in the, hope that it may help to clear...   New Age/Religion Pages 646

Abandonment To Divine Providence *by Jean-Pierre de Caussade*   ISBN: *1-59462-228-0*   **$25.95**
"The Rev. Jean Pierre de Caussade was one of the most remarkable spiritual writers of the Society of Jesus in France in the 18th Century. His death took place at Toulouse in 1751. His works have gone through many editions and have been republished...   Inspirational/Religion Pages 400

Mental Chemistry *by Charles Haanel*   ISBN: *1-59462-192-6*   **$23.95**
Mental Chemistry allows the change of material conditions by combining and appropriately utilizing the power of the mind. Much like applied chemistry creates something new and unique out of careful combinations of chemicals the mastery of mental chemistry...   New Age Pages 354

The Letters of Robert Browning and Elizabeth Barret Barrett 1845-1846 vol II   ISBN: *1-59462-193-4*   **$35.95**
by Robert Browning and Elizabeth Barrett   Biographies Pages 596

Gleanings In Genesis (volume I) *by Arthur W. Pink*   ISBN: *1-59462-130-6*   **$27.45**
Appropriately has Genesis been termed "the seed plot of the Bible" for in it we have, in germ form, almost all of the great doctrines which are afterwards fully developed in the books of Scripture which follow...   Religion/Inspirational Pages 420

The Master Key *by L. W. de Laurence*   ISBN: *1-59462-001-6*   **$30.95**
In no branch of human knowledge has there been a more lively increase of the spirit of research during the past few years than in the study of Psychology, Concentration and Mental Discipline. The requests for authentic lessons in Thought Control, Mental Discipline and...   New Age/Business Pages 422

The Lesser Key Of Solomon Goetia *by L. W. de Laurence*   ISBN: *1-59462-092-X*   **$9.95**
This translation of the first book of the "Lernegton" which is now for the first time made accessible to students of Talismanic Magic was done, after careful collation and edition, from numerous Ancient Manuscripts in Hebrew, Latin, and French...   New Age/Occult Pages 92

Rubaiyat Of Omar Khayyam *by Edward Fitzgerald*   ISBN:*1-59462-332-5*   **$13.95**
Edward Fitzgerald, whom the world has already learned, in spite of his own efforts to remain within the shadow of anonymity, to look upon as one of the rarest poets of the century, was born at Bredfield, in Suffolk, on the 31st of March, 1809. He was the third son of John Purcell...   Music Pages 172

Ancient Law *by Henry Maine*   ISBN: *1-59462-128-4*   **$29.95**
The chief object of the following pages is to indicate some of the earliest ideas of mankind, as they are reflected in Ancient Law, and to point out the relation of those ideas to modern thought.   Religion/History Pages 452

Far-Away Stories *by William J. Locke*   ISBN: *1-59462-129-2*   **$19.45**
"Good wine needs no bush, but a collection of mixed vintages does. And this book is just such a collection. Some of the stories I do not want to remain buried for ever in the museum files of dead magazine-numbers an author's not unpardonable vanity..."   Fiction Pages 272

Life of David Crockett *by David Crockett*   ISBN: *1-59462-250-7*   **$27.45**
"Colonel David Crockett was one of the most remarkable men of the times in which he lived. Born in humble life, but gifted with a strong will, an indomitable courage, and unremitting perseverance...   Biographies/New Age Pages 424

Lip-Reading *by Edward Nitchie*   ISBN: *1-59462-206-X*   **$25.95**
Edward B. Nitchie, founder of the New York School for the Hard of Hearing, now the Nitchie School of Lip-Reading, Inc, wrote "LIP-READING Principles and Practice". The development and perfecting of this meritorious work on lip-reading was an undertaking...   How-to Pages 400

A Handbook of Suggestive Therapeutics, Applied Hypnotism, Psychic Science   ISBN: *1-59462-214-0*   **$24.95**
by Henry Munro   Health/New Age/Health/Self-help Pages 376

A Doll's House: and Two Other Plays *by Henrik Ibsen*   ISBN: *1-59462-112-8*   **$19.95**
Henrik Ibsen created this classic when in revolutionary 1848 Rome. Introducing some striking concepts in playwriting for the realist genre, this play has been studied the world over.   Fiction/Classics/Plays 308

The Light of Asia *by sir Edwin Arnold*   ISBN: *1-59462-204-3*   **$13.95**
In this poetic masterpiece, Edwin Arnold describes the life and teachings of Buddha. The man who was to become known as Buddha to the world was born as Prince Gautama of India but he rejected the worldly riches and abandoned the reigns of power when...   Religion/History/Biographies Pages 170

The Complete Works of Guy de Maupassant *by Guy de Maupassant*   ISBN: *1-59462-157-8*   **$16.95**
"For days and days, nights and nights, I had dreamed of that first kiss which was to consecrate our engagement, and I knew not on what spot I should put my lips..."   Fiction/Classics Pages 240

The Art of Cross-Examination *by Francis L. Wellman*   ISBN: *1-59462-309-0*   **$26.95**
Written by a renowned trial lawyer, Wellman imparts his experience and uses case studies to explain how to use psychology to extract desired information through questioning.   How-to/Science/Reference Pages 408

Answered or Unanswered? *by Louisa Vaughan*   ISBN: *1-59462-248-5*   **$10.95**
Miracles of Faith in China   Religion Pages 112

The Edinburgh Lectures on Mental Science (1909) *by Thomas*   ISBN: *1-59462-008-3*   **$11.95**
This book contains the substance of a course of lectures recently given by the writer in the Queen Street Hall, Edinburgh. Its purpose is to indicate the Natural Principles governing the relation between Mental Action and Material Conditions...   New Age/Psychology Pages 148

Ayesha *by H. Rider Haggard*   ISBN: *1-59462-301-5*   **$24.95**
Verily and indeed it is the unexpected that happens! Probably if there was one person upon the earth from whom the Editor of this, and of a certain previous history, did not expect to hear again...   Classics Pages 380

Ayala's Angel *by Anthony Trollope*   ISBN: *1-59462-352-X*   **$29.95**
The two girls were both pretty, but Lucy who was twenty-one who supposed to be simple and comparatively unattractive, whereas Ayala was credited, as her Bombwhat romantic name might show, with poetic charm and a taste for romance. Ayala when her father died was nineteen...   Fiction Pages 484

The American Commonwealth *by James Bryce*   ISBN: *1-59462-286-8*   **$34.45**
An interpretation of American democratic political theory. It examines political mechanics and society from the perspective of Scotsman James Bryce   Politics Pages 572

Stories of the Pilgrims *by Margaret P. Pumphrey*   ISBN: *1-59462-116-0*   **$17.95**
This book explores pilgrims religious oppression in England as well as their escape to Holland and eventual crossing to America on the Mayflower, and their early days in New England...   History Pages 268

QTY

The Fasting Cure *by Sinclair Upton*   ISBN: *1-59462-222-1*   **$13.95**
In the Cosmopolitan Magazine for May, 1910, and in the Contemporary Review (London) for April, 1910, I published an article dealing with my experiences in fasting. I have written a great many magazine articles, but never one which attracted so much attention... New Age/Self Help/Health Pages 164

Hebrew Astrology *by Sepharial*   ISBN: *1-59462-308-2*   **$13.45**
In these days of advanced thinking it is a matter of common observation that we have left many of the old landmarks behind and that we are now pressing forward to greater heights and to a wider horizon than that which represented the mind-content of our progenitors...   Astrology Pages 144

Thought Vibration or The Law of Attraction in the Thought World   ISBN: *1-59462-127-6*   **$12.95**
by William Walker Atkinson   *Psychology/Religion Pages 144*

Optimism *by Helen Keller*   ISBN: *1-59462-108-X*   **$15.95**
Helen Keller was blind, deaf, and mute since 19 months old, yet famously learned how to overcome these handicaps, communicate with the world, and spread her lectures promoting optimism. An inspiring read for everyone...   Biographies/Inspirational Pages 84

Sara Crewe *by Frances Burnett*   ISBN: *1-59462-360-0*   **$9.45**
In the first place, Miss Minchin lived in London. Her home was a large, dull, tall one, in a large, dull square, where all the houses were alike, and all the sparrows were alike, and where all the door-knockers made the same heavy sound...   Childrens/Classic Pages 88

The Autobiography of Benjamin Franklin *by Benjamin Franklin*   ISBN: *1-59462-135-7*   **$24.95**
The Autobiography of Benjamin Franklin has probably been more extensively read than any other American historical work, and no other book of its kind has had such ups and downs of fortune. Franklin lived for many years in England, where he was agent...   Biographies/History Pages 332

Name	
Email	
Telephone	
Address	
City, State ZIP	

☐ **Credit Card**   ☐ **Check / Money Order**

Credit Card Number	
Expiration Date	
Signature	

Please Mail to: Book Jungle
PO Box 2226
Champaign, IL 61825
or Fax to: 630-214-0564

ORDERING INFORMATION

web: *www.bookjungle.com*
email: *sales@bookjungle.com*
fax: *630-214-0564*
mail: *Book Jungle PO Box 2226 Champaign, IL 61825*
or PayPal *to sales@bookjungle.com*

Please contact us for bulk discounts

DIRECT-ORDER TERMS

**20% Discount if You Order
Two or More Books**
Free Domestic Shipping!
Accepted: Master Card, Visa,
Discover, American Express

www.ingramcontent.com/pod-product-compliance
Lightning Source LLC
LaVergne TN
LVHW081326060426
835511LV00011B/1886